What COVID Couldn't Stop

An Advent Devotional:

Putting the Pandemic in Perspective by Focusing on an Unchangeable God

Written by Robert J. LaCosta

No Reputation Communications, LLC
Publishing
1604 River Road
Selkirk, NY 12158
norepcom@gmail.com • 1-844-434-3277

Contents

Spring

The First Candle & Season: Hope
Spring Introduction : Where were You?

Sunday: St Patrick Doesn't Drink Corona
Monday: Easter's Opposite: Ultimate Social Distancing
Tuesday: Masked Apathy
Wednesday: Webcam Into Heaven
Thursday: COVID Gardens & The Unseen Bully
Friday: Love Goes Viral - The Quint-Essential Song
Saturday: How The Daffodils Moved Us Deep Inside

Summer
The Second Candle & Season: Peace
Summer Introduction: Peace Eludes

Sunday: Things That Matter Aren't 'Things.'
Monday: Opposites Attract or Attack
Tuesday: Default to a Sage - Not Rage
Wednesday: Is The Media Your Bible?
Thursday: From Spring Crocus To An Autumn Crocus
Friday: COVID & The Crossbars of Faith
Saturday: The Poignancy of Labor Day, 2020

Contents

Autumn

The Third Candle & Season: Joy
Autumn Introduction: Trees of The Fields Clapped Their Hands

Sunday: Cupid Bests COVID in The Third Round
Monday: Fall + Flu = Fear
Tuesday: COVID Couldn't Take a Bite Out of American Apple Pie
Wednesday: COVID Couldn't Change Colors
Thursday: COVID Couldn't Stop The Sabbath
Friday: COVID Couldn't Stop All Saints
Saturday: Is God Still King During COVID & The Election Cycle?

Winter

The Fourth Candle & Season: Love
It Was a Cold, COVID Night

Winter Introduction: The Vaccine Is Already Here
Sunday: COVID vs. The Covenant Keeper
Monday: COVID vs. The Second Coming Covenant
Tuesday: COVID Couldn't Stop Wise Men
Wednesday: Wise Men Still Seek Him
Christmas Eve: The Longest 'Night'
Christmas Day: Stable Stability

About The Author

More Works by The Author

What COVID Couldn't Stop
- Putting the Pandemic in Perspective by Focusing on an Unchangeable God

Written by Robert J. LaCosta

COVER ART: Frank Romeo
EDITS: Rob Brill

Interior candle photograph by JIM SALITSKY.

Dedication

To those who hurt.

To those who helped others
who were hurting.

To those who hope.

To those who want to see love
go viral more than they want
to be right.

Introduction
Did COVID test 'Positive?'

Is it possible to be in the holiday spirit in 2020?

Putting the pandemic in perspective by focusing on unchangeables is a needed discipline in western culture where we almost expect a drive-thru vaccine for a drive-by virus.

Without minimizing the suffering imposed by the coronavirus with pollyanna anecdotes, these real-time pandemic portals may put you in the holiday spirit after all.

The concept of a daily devotional* and/or Advent devotional is to draw us to God. Period. People of faith cannot put conditions on God to either produce…or else. Would a runner be a true competitor if he decided the steep elevation in front of him wasn't fair?

Join the uphill journey through this "unprecedented" Advent, the season that changes each of us with the unchangeable love of God…even in 2020.

***For a year-round daily devotional that will inspire and teach you how to sense portals to heaven in-the-moment, use "Portals to Heaven" as your devotional in 2021.**

Love Goes Viral

Words and Music by Robert J. LaCosta

The aide comes from Ghana, he's Brooklyn bred
His heart's barely beating, she stays by his bed
during the greatest fight he'll ever weather
from across the globe, they're in this together

CHORUS:
Love goes viral - it's who we're meant to be
In the image of God who heals to set free
Love goes viral though lockdowns constrain
for love lives... from the inside out anyway

The doc's Asian heart has Ivy League smarts
his nurse, she shines bright, she's whiter than white
Their courage must win over their dark fright
About their aging moms when they get back tonight

In their small town, a sad rumor spread
Their beloved Ed was on his deathbed
The cop stops for take-out, confirmed it, but then said,
"The church may be closed but Heaven opened for Ed."

Eager brides and grads may have to wait
as the doting fams plan a great new date
there'll come a time when all of this is past
for love runs ahead – it's the only thing that lasts

BRIDGE:
Quarantines won't dampen the promised vaccines
laboratories of love speed the microscope's dreams
Like daffodils that trumpet the victory of Spring
while the doc heals a laboring lung
That's the love song being sung

1

Spring

The Candle & Season of Hope

Where Were You?

Do you remember first hearing about the coronavirus? COVID-19 was probably somewhere where you weren't. It was distant until it was distant no more.

I was supposed to be in a New York City hospital on March 5 for a spinal fusion operation. By God's leading, I instead took off Presidents Week. The surgeon's office called and said they had a cancellation for February 20th. Bingo. I took it and was released from that Manhattan facility on February 21st. Later, I would thank God endlessly on how those events unfolded in my favor.

Other wonders would flow out of heartbreak and it was these that inspired me to write "Love Goes Viral."

What about you? What happened to you as the crisis became real in Spring 2020?

11

Putting The Unchangeables Into Your Own Words...

Sunday

St. Patrick Doesn't Drink Corona

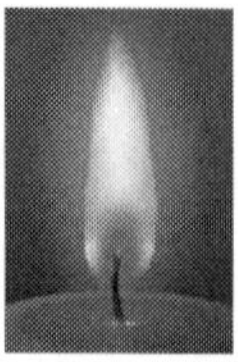

St. Patrick's Day fell off The Cliffs of Moher or so it seemed in 2020. Confidence, in general, plummeted.

It's natural to think about circumstances, troubles and tragedies in the light of Providence. Did God allow the coronavirus? Did Satan cause it?

There are those who would assign it to the category of a "discipline" on our powerful and prosperous America – sort of like David's plague caused by his nationalistic pride. It would be easy to fall into that camp except that other countries have been experiencing worse issues than us. Does that make them wickeder than America?

In the Old Testament, a couple of plagues were stopped by angels. In those incidents, God judged rebellion and pride.

When St. Patrick was 16, he was kidnapped. Later, he wrote that it was a judgment upon him and his countrymen. Yet, when it was all said and done, God used that horrific act to save a country.

Because none of us really know the answers (although some will purport that they do), it would be well to return to some of the vibrant sureties that are found in "St. Patrick's Breastplate;" one of Christianity's most exhilarating and fear-busting prayers. In it, he expresses:

That our God is a mighty Trinity…that Christ has defeated death…that the Holy Spirit is our holy formal seal of promise…that saints have been courageous before us…that angels – like the ones who were ordered to stop plagues – are all about us. And so forth and so on.

We don't know all the answers in these swings of providential circumstances. But we do know The One who holds the answers; The One St. Patrick said he prayed to "one hundred times a day and almost as many in the night" through snow, frost and rain as he tended sheep.

If the coronavirus drives us to our knees as Patrick's woes did for him, then let us rest upon the thought that prayer is always the timely and most potent vaccine.

PORTAL TO HEAVEN: We don't have to understand all of God's ways in order to draw nearer to Him.

Satan rose up against Israel and incited David to take a census of Israel... So the Lord sent a plague on Israel, and seventy thousand men of Israel fell dead. Then David said to God, "I have sinned greatly by doing this. Now, I beg you, take away the guilt of your servant. I have done a very foolish thing."... And God sent an angel to destroy Jerusalem. But as the angel was doing so, the Lord saw it and relented concerning the disaster and said to the angel who was destroying the people, "Enough! Withdraw your hand."...You meant evil against me, but God meant it for good, to bring it about that many people should be kept alive, as they are today.
1 Chronicles 21:1,14,8,15, NIV Genesis 50:20, ESV

Monday

Easter's Opposite: Ultimate Social Distancing

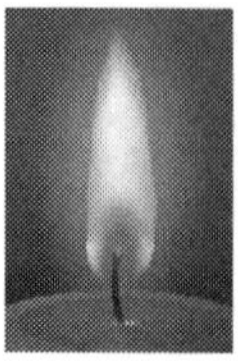

If we thought social distancing was tough in 2020, imagine how Jesus experienced it and spoke of it throughout his life.

He talked of hard hearts that separated stiff-necked leaders and people from the love he brought from his Father. (See John 5:24-47)

He was thrown out of his hometown synagogue. Can you imagine forced social-distancing from your tight-knit faith community?

For crying out loud, authorities wouldn't even let him die in Jerusalem. They "distanced" him to expire on the cross outside the city.

It is easy to find social-distance-ers of Jesus today. They want nothing to do with him and especially his followers.

In eternity, Jesus will let them have their own way.

PORTAL TO HEAVEN: Religious instruction for children teaches that hell is "eternal separation from God" who is the source of all goodness. How nightmarish to be forever trapped with your own hard-heart and like-minded folks. That just might be worse than the licking flames.

Most assuredly, I say to you, he who hears My word and believes in Him who sent Me has everlasting life, and shall not come into judgment, but has passed from death into life...[My Father] has given [Me] authority to execute judgment...you do not have his word abiding in you, because whom He sent, Him you do not believe...you are not willing to come to Me that you may have life.
John 5:24,27,38,40 NKJV [Brackets for brevity]

Tuesday

Masked Apathy?

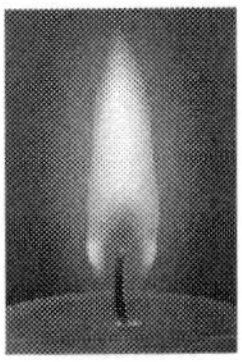

Masks make it easier to apathetically pass by someone.

After all, we don't want to catch what they might have.

People are actually veering right or left to avoid each other, literally and figuratively taking us out of step with each other.

If we're not careful, the idea of avoiding glances and interaction could become second nature and that's not a new normal that anyone should welcome.

It's possible that we've always been social distancing.

Do we notice a person in need that we run across? If we know them, do we ask if there's something specific that they could use? Some of the "marginalized" are fairly obvious. Do we lend a hand?

Or, do we veer to the right or left so as to not "catch" their needy glance?

PORTAL TO HEAVEN: Jesus didn't veer away from our planet to avoid catching what we have.

Suppose you see a brother or sister who has no food or clothing, and you say, "Good-bye and have a good day; stay warm and eat well"—but then you don't give that person any food or clothing. What good does that do? So you see, faith by itself isn't enough. Unless it produces good deeds, it is dead and useless...Jesus reached out his hand and touched the man. "I am willing," he said.
James 2:15-17 NLT, 1 John 3:17 NLT, Matthew 8:3 NIV

Wednesday

Webcam Into Heaven

Call the timing of my visions of heaven "Corona Chimera," but springtime is how I envision heaven eternally. Birds singing, flowers blooming, scents wafting and temperatures that all can agree to…

When the time comes, I'll ask Adam and Eve if the Garden of Eden refused the other three seasons.

For now, it's "Corona Current" and I can only dream about springtime's bloom being the ultimate metaphor for the resurrection of our health and finances.

One great hope of spring is the cherry blossoms. Washington D.C.'s trees have long overshadowed a park in Newark, New Jersey that has seen everything from racial disturbances to the festivities called the Cherry Blossom Festival.

Branch Brook Park boasts some of the loveliest scenes you can imagine every April. Corona closed it.

But Essex County ingeniously used

webcam technology to give us a window into different views of the park and promised that 2021 would be worth waiting for.

Whether you're simply enmeshed in getting past the corona drama or looking forward to heaven when there will be "no more death or mourning or crying or pain" (Revelation 21:4 NIV), Branch Brook Park's webcam welcomes a season that speaks to either or both.

PORTAL TO HEAVEN: The webcam opens up literal contemporary and eternal portals. Are you looking for them?

He will wipe every tear from their eyes. There will be no more death or mourning or crying or pain, for the old order of things has passed away... He who was seated on the throne said, "I am making everything new!" Then he said, "Write this down, for these words are trustworthy and true."
Revelation 21:4,5 NIV

Thursday

COVID Gardens & The Unseen Bully

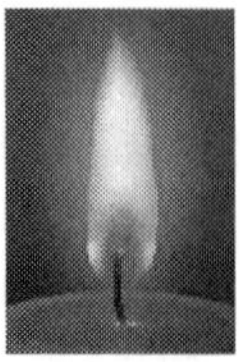

The corona crisis produced growth in so many of us… literally. Throughout the country, COVID gardens abounded.

I named mine "The COVID Garden" so that every time I walked by it, I would remember that God causes growth in the valleys. It represented a refusal to be intimidated by the unseen viral bully. It was a deliberate move in the opposite spirit of the prevailing times.

In the future, guests and grandchildren yet-to-be-born will see the strength and beauty of the flowers and vegetables. Yet, they won't know the backstory.

Isn't that the metaphorical X-ray of the character of every person who allows God to work through their hard times?

PORTAL TO HEAVEN: Christ taught us how to climb a seemingly impossible hill to victory.

You are our letter. You are written in our hearts. You are known and read by all men. You are as a letter from Christ...Not only so, but we also glory in our sufferings, because we know that suffering produces perseverance; perseverance, character; and character, hope...consider it pure joy, my brothers and sisters, whenever you face trials of many kinds, because you know that the testing of your faith produces perseverance. Let perseverance finish its work so that you may be mature and complete, not lacking anything...do not be surprised at the fiery ordeal that has come on you to test you, as though something strange were happening to you...But rejoice inasmuch as you participate in the sufferings of Christ, so that you may be overjoyed when his glory is revealed.
2 Corinthians 3:2,3 NLV, Romans 5:3,4 NIV, James 1:2-4 NIV, 1 Peter 4:12,13 NIV

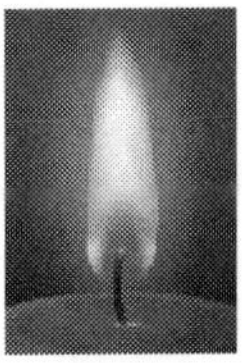

Putting The Unchangeables Into Your Own Words...

Friday

'Love Goes Viral:'
The Quint-'Essential' Song by The Essential Worker*

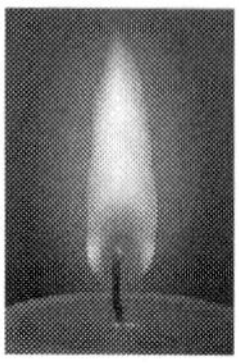

COVID affected me the most as a hearing instrument specialist, a writer and a son-in-law.

The latter role gave me the opportunity to spend three months with my mother-in-law under my roof. That was one of the greatest privileges of my life. It was as if time was standing still and it made up for all of the other years that a busy schedule frustrated my desire to get together with her at her house for a cup of coffee or to watch one of the old movies that she loved.

In terms of the first role as an essential worker, hearing became more critical than ever as people spent more time together constantly watching televisions turned up way too loud! Seriously, hearing impairment frustrates everyone, especially in close-quarter lockdowns.

With regard to my work as a writer, my heart was stirred more than ever as I witnessed acts of courage and love nearby and around the world. It was in the midst of the pandemic that I penned *Love Goes Viral*, a song that celebrates love-in-action. I termed it "The Quint-Essential Song by the Essential Worker."

I wanted a hope-filled, snap-shot COVID memorial song minus any superficiality. This cut cuts deep into my soul because I were living it out while I wrote it out. I personally lived with the concern of giving my mother-in-law the virus when I returned from work. It was heart wrenching to watch my stepdaughter postpone her wedding twice. Two of my daughter's businesses were shut down. My sister was unable to get critical eye surgery that left her legally blind. Some of these events became part of the song's lyrical montage.

Even so, I wanted to embed inspirational imagery in an upbeat song that would evoke a desire for listeners to choose love over fear while tapping their toes.

The country-pop chorus underscores the worldwide lesson that courage can't be locked down while the music video powerfully portrays love in triumph across generational, ethnic and national borders. The catchy chorus rides along without skimping on simple profundity:

'Love goes viral, it's who we're meant to be. In the image of God who heals to set free. Love goes viral, though lockdowns constrain, for love lives from the inside out anyway.'
(From *Love Goes Viral* ©2020 Robert J. LaCosta)

PORTAL TO HEAVEN: Whenever I listen to or watch *Love Goes Viral* on YouTube, it makes me consider that COVID was essential in some ironic way.

Don't let evil conquer you, but conquer evil by doing good… The LORD has made everything for its own purpose, Even the wicked for the day of evil… "I have told you these things, so that in me you may have peace. In this world you will have trouble. But take heart! I have overcome the world."
Romans 12:12 NLT, Proverbs 16:4 NLT, John 16:33 NIV

** "Love Goes Viral" is on iTunes or other streaming services. View on YouTube or order it from lovegoesviral.us The lyrics are at the beginning of this book.*

Saturday

How The Daffodils Moved Us Deep Inside

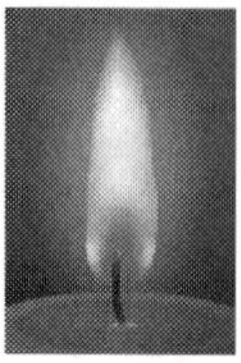

The vase of daffodils on the dining room is a portal I'll always treasure.

During the midst of the pandemic in spring, the little well house was buffeted by the best blooms we'd ever had since moving onto the property. The daffodils had become our symbols of hope.

After an unusual late april overnight ice storm, we awoke to bowed beauties with dirt on some of their faces.

I was as crushed as they looked.

I rushed out there first thing in the morning to find that many were irreversibly bent. It was like going to a wake. I finally accepted it and snapped them at the point of the petal where the 90-degree crease occurred.

Next, I lifted each of the surviving daffodils as they had lifted me. The crystals of ice fought me each step of the way, but I would not let them have their say. I carefully shook the slush from the base. I curved some flowers around other's petals so they could not droop.

After this painstaking process, I gathered the broken and tenderly washed each delicate trumpet and placed them in a vase more carefully than any florist.

Over the next few days, I realized that this portal to heaven summarized what had been happening in many hearts during the pandemic. A storm had tried to take away the outside beauty of our cultures only to brighten our tables within as households reacquainted themselves with the things that matter – like a family gathered for a meal around an exquisite centerpiece of daffodils.

PORTAL TO HEAVEN: There isn't a situation that God cannot show Himself - especially during crises.

And we know that for those who love God all things work together for good, for those who are called according to his purpose... You intended to harm me, but God intended it all for good.
Romans 8:28 ESV, Genesis 50:20 NLT

2

Summer

The Candle
& Season of Peace

Just One Little Piece of Peace, Please

As Spring turned the corner, news of COVID restrictions being lightened spread as fast as the virus. Some may have jumped the gun, but everyone in northern climates was glad to get out of their houses on a more regular basis.

As temperatures climbed, were you still worried that your body's temperature would also peak? Were you disappointed about a vacation, travel or something as simple as touching a basketball or baseball or restaurant door?

The second Advent candle symbolizes peace.

Besides the anxiety of the pandemic, another viral infection ramped up in the form of racism, in the wake of the killing of an African American named George Floyd by a Minnesota police officer. The heat of the moment triggered riots and take-overs. Peace was not exactly flowing in the streets of American cities.

Unfortunately, both the virus and Floyd's death served to escalate an already heated political cycle and thus the "triple-threat" of the summer of 2020 was in full swing.

The church of Jesus Christ was faced with a decision and many within the Body of Christ chose the right answer. They would push through racial barriers and work for toward reforms and peaceful solutions.

Whenever Jesus wanted to give us peace, He reassured us. During the summer months, there were some beautiful, almost mesmerizing signs that Jesus was comforting us through obvious portals - many of which came through the summer season itself.

It might be good to reflect on some of the remembrances during the summer months.

Sunday

Things That Matter Aren't 'Things'

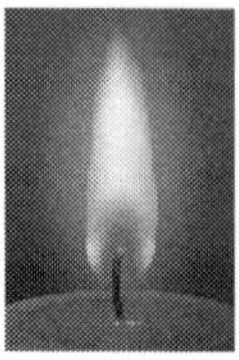

Certain restrictions began to lift in June and it became clear that my wife's aging mother with pre-existing conditions could now return home after sheltering in place with us for three months.

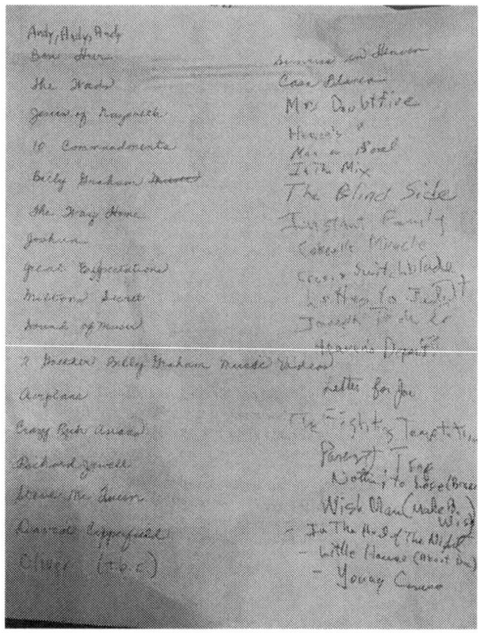

Throughout the spring, we had watched our share of her favorite reruns and began to intimately understand why Andy Griffith got so frustrated with Barney. Around Easter, we had enjoyed *Jesus of Nazareth*, *Ben Hur*, *The Ten Commandments* and *The Sound of Music*. All tolled, forty movies literally burned out the screen on our television.

Still, the best comedy and drama happened in our living room and at our dining room table for three, count 'em three, square meals together. No running out the door. Not a lot of interruptions. We even had time for Mom's sweet tooth as desserts were served every time.

Sitting next to her on the couch, teasing each other, helping with her meds and meals and going for walks-and-talks became the norm I had wished for over the past 14 years.

In God's divine wisdom, a lot of life that had been missed got squeezed into three months.

We had been more than a little concerned that COVID could infect Mom and take her away. Instead, it brought her to us.

PORTAL TO HEAVEN: The presents of presence can come wrapped and it's up to us to unwrap them and thank The Giftgiver.

And we know that for those who love God all things work together for good, for those who are called according to his purpose.
Romans 8:28 NASB

Monday

Opposites Attract!

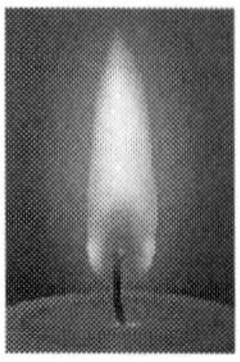

Opposites attract!

In the midst of the pandemic, racial unrest was added.

Inflated and inflamed because it was an election year, we might ask, "What's a person to do?"

Do the opposite.

When egged on, don't take the bait. It's natural to want to take up the gauntlet because we not only want to BE right, we want the challenger to admit that we ARE right.

To not be drawn into the argument might make us appear as the weak one or, worse yet, the surrendered one.

The kingdom of God is absolutely the upside-down world where a "gentle answer turns back wrath" and evil is overcome with good as kindness spreads ashes on the head of the attacker.

During an election year that causes us to walk on eggshells or get egged on, it appears that opposites can either attack or attract.

PORTAL TO HEAVEN: Might God be using this volatile social unrest as a portal to heaven; a way of showing us that the upside-down looks pretty good from where He is sitting?

A gentle answer turns away wrath, but a harsh word stirs up anger...Jesus said, "My kingdom is not of this world. If it were, my servants would fight to prevent my arrest by the Jewish leaders. But now my kingdom is from another place."..When the king of Israel saw them, he asked Elisha, "Shall I kill them, my father? Shall I kill them?" "Do not kill them," he answered. "Would you kill those you have captured with your own sword or bow? Set food

and water before them so that they may eat and drink and then go back to their master." So he prepared a great feast for them, and after they had finished eating and drinking, he sent them away, and they returned to their master. So the bands from Aram stopped raiding Israel's territory…"I am leaving you with a gift—peace of mind and heart. And the peace I give is a gift the world cannot give. So don't be troubled or afraid."

Proverbs 15:1 NIV, John 18:36 NIV, 2 Kings 6:21 NIV, John 14:27 NLT

Tuesday

Default to a Sage, Not Rage

Anger is one of the fastest solvents for stripping discussion of godliness.

It happens when one or both spouses lose their temper. What prevails is someone sleeping on the couch. It occurs when children or teens get into a spat and start dividing their friends.

And it happened during the riots and protests during 2020.

The late pastor and philosophy professor Dallas Willard said:

"How to stand for what is right without anger…Many people think they cannot stand for what is right unless they are angry. We live in a society that is sick with anger over issues of justice. There's plenty to be mad about. Think about things that humans do to one another."

If we put this in the context of the horrific killing of George Floyd, we should ask, "How could one person do that to another and how could one not be enraged over that act?"

But the wise sage gives us some instruction that may have saved lives, broken hearts and broken windows, millions and millions of dollars and a further division among groups.

Dallas, on what God taught him:

"Jesus says anger won't help. But there is standard teaching in the world that if you're not angry over conditions, you must be brain dead. So, I have to go to Jesus and let him teach me about that.

"If I'm in a situation where there might be anger, I have to listen to the gentle voice of God. Here is something Jesus taught me: Everything you can accomplish with anger, you can accomplish much better without it. You don't have to be angry to stand for what is right. And if you do stand for what is right in anger, you will deflect the people involved from the real issue and they'll just be mad at you. Anger elicits more anger.

"Anger isn't a sin, but if you hang on to it, it will lead you there. 'Anger rests in the bosom of fools.' The Book of Ecclesiastes tells us. It doesn't mean that if you're angry, you are a fool. It means that if you want to find a lot of anger, go find a fool.

(Continued)

Tuesday

Default to a Sage, Not Rage (Continued)

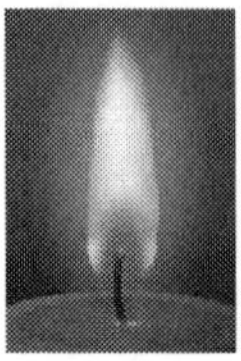

(Continued)

"If you want to stand for what is right, do it without anger, and that will help them come to grips with the issue. If you come at it with anger, they will tie onto your anger and forget the issue.

"Anger is like pain; it calls attention to something that's wrong and that's good. Once you've had your attention called to it, you need to deal with it on the basis of love and not anger.

"Anger sets love aside. Love works for what is good and not just what I want to see happen to them because I'm angry at them. Anger is the will to harm or at least a readiness to see someone harmed. We have to come to these understandings from the inside and that's where Jesus works with us."

In this time, may God lead us to a sage instead of rage.

PORTAL TO HEAVEN: Hearing God and gaining His wisdom requires a will to listen to Him.

This is what the LORD says: "Stand at the crossroads and look; ask for the ancient paths, ask where the good way is, and walk in it, and you will find rest for your soul"...And "don't sin by letting anger control you." Don't let the sun go down while you are still angry, and do not give the devil a foothold.
Jeremiah 6:16 NIV, Ephesians 4:26,27 NLT

Wednesday

Is The Media Your Bible?

Images on television and social media are intended to inflame us.

How does making us angry at people we don't even know help the media sell ads and promote their platform?

Media reports on TV and smart phones indulge the flesh. Our sinful nature actually likes anger or even fury.

One fleshy piece of news after another gets us on the edge of our seat to salivate more than any fictional account ever could. Bingo! They've got us.

True freedom is so personal. We are free to shut off that which feeds the flesh and deliberately turn to God to feed our spirit. It's one of the beautiful things about Psalm 23 and other scriptures that tell us, "Life in Me is not spinning out of control for I am with you." The Good Shepherd, leading us through the shadow of death, then asks,"Are you with Me?"

Once we've turned off that which inflames and turn on that which gives life, we are "free" to love.

PORTAL TO HEAVEN: The road to Calvary was filled with audible hatred and visual imagery that could have inflamed Jesus. He used it to serve the opposite purpose.

You, my brothers and sisters, were called to be free. But do not use your freedom to indulge the flesh; rather, serve one another humbly in love. For the entire law is fulfilled in keeping this one command: "Love your neighbor as yourself."
Galatians 5:18 NIV

Thursday

It Started With A Spring Crocus, Ended With A Fall Crocus

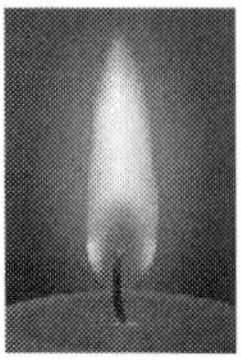

Juxtaposition reigned in 2020.

There was the radical difference between media melancholy and the spirited Mother Nature.

This was the year of color in the most dreary of times.

The spring crocuses and bright daffodils next to our well house were like a child daring to cheer up her mom during a solemn occasion with a picture she drew of flowers.

Not only were these yellow belles more plentiful than any ever, they were courageous in their efforts to fight the virus's dread when a late snowstorm iced them down. They bowed, but never fell.

The wisteria that graced the roof of that same well house would have driven Monet to buy a ticket on the first boat that sailed to visit our yard. Truly, it may have been a once-in-a-lifetimer.

The peonies plotted to upstage the other gardens before the rhododendrons bested any prior years.

Lilacs and spiderworts and autumn crocuses added their touches and the overall effect was a stern rebuke to COVID's colorlessness.

PORTAL TO HEAVEN: It's God's pattern to paint powerful imagery so we can't miss that it all started with His dream of a garden.

If God cares so wonderfully for flowers that are here today and thrown into the fire tomorrow, he will certainly care for you. Why do you have so little faith?...I will be like the dew to Israel; he will blossom like a lily...Flowers appear on the earth; the season of singing has come...

Luke 12:28 NLT, Hosea 14:5 NIV, Song of Solomon 2:12 NIV

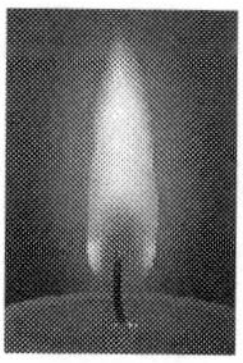

Putting The Unchangeables Into Your Own Words...

Friday

COVID & the Crossbars of Faith

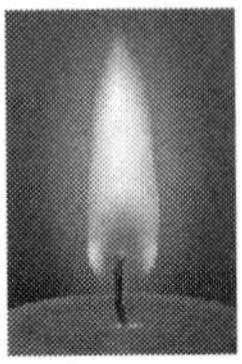

Could beauty come out of COVID?

My immediate thought went to those on the front lines during the pandemic.

It was love in action. Those acts of dedication spurred me to write "Love Goes Viral."
But what could I do from the confines of my office with restricted hours and from the the couch where my mother-in-law was being quarantined?

"Let's take this fight outside," my spirit cried.

So I went out and planted a vegetable patch and a flower garden complete with a faux small black wrought iron fencing. For the first time since we moved here, we had a British touch with the flowers and an Italian influence over on the veggie side.

We took out the tractor and moved a seven-foot rhododendron bush and a tender hibiscus plant. We mulched.

Months later, when we needed to quarantine for 14 days after traveling, the vegetarian in our home was without vegetables. That ain't right. Lo and behold, our COVID garden chose that very day to produce our initial zucchini and tomatoes. A few hours later, my brother-in-law coincidently brought over a couple of bags of other vegetables including, of course, the aromatic 'basanagol' which turned into the best pandemic pesto sauce in the world.

But when I walk by the COVID flower garden, I have mixed emotions as I remember that beauty must often be wrought out of pain.

That's the juxtaposition of the two rough pieces of wood that intersect the vertical of heaven with the horizontal of earth. The vertical had to be firmly on the ground and The Lover had to spread his arms on the horizontal.

PORTAL TO HEAVEN: Suffering and joy are the crossbars of faith.

We do this by keeping our eyes on Jesus, the champion who initiates and perfects our faith. Because of the joy awaiting him, he endured the cross, disregarding its shame. Now he is seated in the place of honor beside God's throne.
Hebrews 12:2 NLT

Saturday

The Poignancy of Labor Day 2020

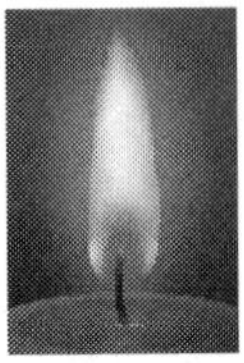

Rising to a stunning Labor Day sunrise, I realized once again that there are beautiful happenings every day of our lives.

The pandemic wrestled with our wits. We didn't let it pin us.

Labor Day was especially poignant during 2020 as we honored both "essential" and "non-essential" workers. (If all honest labor is sacred, are there really any "non-essential" workers?)

The Good Book tells us to enjoy our labor.

Labor Day reminds us that the grocery store checkout lady and the guy behind the counter at the convenience store are never to be taken for granted. They were clerks-turned-heroes. Health care workers got a morale-boosting shot-in-the-arm.

Other folks not to be ignored were those who raised awareness and oversaw non-profits as these were particularly hard hit by COVID. Their fund-raisers were cancelled or postponed.

Perhaps Thanksgiving and Christmastime could help them make up for what was lost in 2020 if we take some of what we earned from our labor and remember those who couldn't.

PORTAL TO HEAVEN: If your heart is in the right place, you won't have to labor too hard to see the beauty in people and places.

May the favor of the Lord our God rest on us; establish the work of our hands for us— yes, establish the work of our hands...Do not work for food that spoils, but for food that endures to eternal life, which the Son of Man will give you. For on him God the Father has placed his seal of approval.
Psalm 90:17 NIV, John 6:27 NIV

3

Autumn

The Candle & Season Of Joy

Questions Fell Like Leaves In The Fall

With predictions that the flu season would again usher in spikes in coronavirus cases, nations braced for the worst.

In America, a presidential election added to the anxiety as a “civil war” of sorts began to divide best friends and families.

Between the pandemic and politics, it was scarier than Halloween.

Within that context, God breathed the most beautiful autumn colors in recent memory. Again, there seemed to be an obvious juxtaposition; one so noticeable that it seemed God was asking the question, “What message do you get from the parallel or fear and suffering and hope and reassurance?”

He didn’t answer that question for us.

CUPID Bests COVID in Third Round

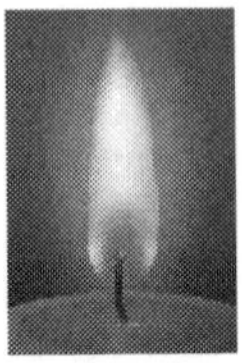

It was as if the altar was at the top of Mt. Everest…

Late April is beautiful in Atlanta and the wedding venue expectantly oozed of an exquisite ceremony.

Like most eager brides, she listened again and again to reports of the coronavirus shutting down one thing after another and shutting down her dream.

Spring is a time of hope, of new growth and budding and all of the symbols of starting a lifetime of love.

But such hope and optimism would have to be put off…indefinitely.

The wedding dress and the bridesmaids' dresses hung in closets instead of gracing excited young women.

When restrictions and predictions seemed to offer a window of hope, a second date was scheduled for the fall, only to have that fall through.

When she finally scaled the pandemic's peak to say her vows, it was in early October. There were no new buds on the trees. Instead, providence provided a different metaphor. Since the third and successful attempt at a ceremony occurred in an Upstate New York vineyard, it was clear that the most luscious and plump purple grapes would be the substitute symbol, as if Jesus had saved the best wine for last.

PORTAL TO HEAVEN: Some portals require squinting.

"Everyone brings out the choice wine first and then the cheaper wine after the guests have had too much to drink; but you have saved the best till now."
John 2:10 NIV

Monday

Fall + Flu = Fear vs. Faith's Mathematics

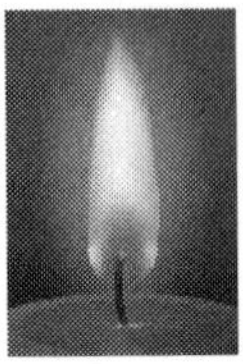

The mathematics of fear and faith have bad results if one is substituted for the other and that is why we need a math teacher.

God isn't an ordinary professor. We must pay attention in class in order to see that His equations always turn out.

With Autumn's flu season approaching, the nations braced for the worse. It is good that we prepare and that people follow safety measures. That's good math!

The other side of the coin is an equation that can infect people and paralyze a country:

Fall + Flu = Fear.

Here are some equations from scripture that work out every time:

Peace I leave + Peace I give = Do not let your hearts be troubled.
John 14:27

I Command + Be strong and courageous and Do not be afraid = I will be with you wherever you go.
Joshua 1:9

Do not worry about tomorrow + Tomorrow has its own worry = Peace for today.
Matthew 6:34

Even though I walk through valley + I will not fear = You comfort me.
Psalm 23:4

Seek Me + I answer = I deliver you from all your fears. Psalm 34:4

Neither death nor the future + anything in creation = can separate me from God.
Romans 8:38,39

The Lord is my light and salvation + The Stronghold of my life = Whom shall I be afraid of?
Psalm 27:1

These are just from Math 101.

PORTAL TO HEAVEN: God has actually given us a choice about fear and faith with the former providing a portal to hell and the latter being a portal to heaven.

Tuesday

COVID Couldn't Take A Bite Out Of American Apple Pie

If you could pick a bright spot during a crisis like COVID, you might want to pick apples.

Orchards are a metaphor of plenty; that God has as many ways of providing as there are varieties of apples. He can load down an apple tree so intensely that it literally bows in worship.

To illustrate His point, He "picked" the pandemic as a bumper year for apples.

And just to add a mixed metaphor of a cherry on top, God tosses a row of golden trees as a backsplash to the orchard.

To sweeten the pie even more, He puts pick-your-own people right in front of such bounty so they can't miss the delicious truth that they are the "apple of his eye."

PORTAL TO HEAVEN: God provides the portals; we simply provide the eyes.

Keep me as the apple of Your eye; hide me under the shadow of Your wings.
Psalm 17:8 NKJV

Wednesday

COVID Couldn't Change Colors

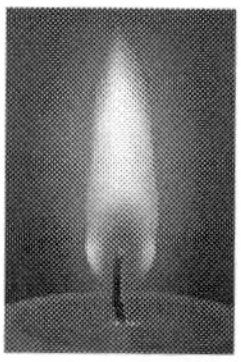

COVID can't change colors.

But God can.

Observing the "illustrious" command of the fall foliage, it begins to be a fixed point of reference.

From one tree's advance in hue to another, the logical progression toward Thanksgiving is tantamount to a storyboard. While peak in our parts happens around Columbus Day, every step along the path of Autumn is like entering a new room at a never-ending museum of magnificence.

By comparison, the latest pandemic media update seems to morph into black and white like a 1950's television set.

PORTAL TO HEAVEN: Some things are so big they make us tremble. Other things are so grand they make us bow.

"While the earth remains, seedtime and harvest, and cold and heat, and summer and winter, and day and night shall not cease."...If you can break My covenant with the day and...night, so that there will not be day and night in their season, [only] then My covenant may also be broken with David..."
Genesis 8:22 NASB, Psalm 33:20,21a NJKV. Editor's bracket.

Thursday

COVID Couldn't Stop the Sabbath

Ironically, COVID couldn't stop a much needed extended "sabbath." In Hebrew, sabbath means "to rest from labor." Workers in lockdown reported closer relationships at home. Smart ones included God in that category.

In scripture, the sabbath is the idea of truly letting go of the belief that we need seven days to meet our financial needs. God does it for us in six. That makes Him God and not us. To rigidly cling to the concept that we need 168 hours each week to care for our lives is tantamount to distrust and rebellion and that's why honoring the sabbath is one of the Ten Commandments...

In an attempt to honor the Sabbath, I wrestled with the idea of not finishing the job of gathering massive leaf piles on a Sunday afternoon before a predicted rainstorm later in the evening.

I was so sorely tempted that I made a few attempts of walking toward the barn to get the tractor out and break my Sabbath. Each time, I stopped in my tracks.

I finally decided that there was still a slight chance that it wouldn't rain overnight and tomorrow might afford me the opportunity to make a dent in the forty acre mess we call "Autumn."

Monday came. I awoke to soaked leaves. It appeared that sabbath-keeping backfired.

However, at 3 pm, my nodding head over my desk and slouched body woke me up to the fact that I needed a break from writing this very book. I headed outdoors and attacked the trees' teardrops. Within a few hours, I realized I had gotten an unexpected sabbath from writing. I got some needed fresh autumn air. I also raked in a podcast on my headphones while riding the mower and its topic just happened to be about the sabbath.

PORTAL TO HEAVEN: It is when we find that things that somehow fall into place in six days that help us relent to the fact that God really does know what He's doing. The recharging of the body, mind and spirit laborless-ly earns us a portal into His goodness and brilliance.

There remains, then, a Sabbath-rest for the people of God; for anyone who enters God's rest also rests from their works, just as God did from his. Let us, therefore, make every effort to enter that rest, so that no one will perish by following their example of disobedience...See to it, brothers and sisters, that none of you has a sinful, unbelieving heart that turns away from the living God...Observe the Sabbath day, to keep it holy. Work six days and do everything you need to do. But the seventh day is a Sabbath to God, your God. Don't do any work—not you, nor your son, nor your daughter, nor your servant, nor your maid, nor your animals, not even the foreign guest visiting in your town. For in six days God made Heaven, Earth, and sea, and everything in them; he rested on the seventh day. Therefore God blessed the Sabbath day; he set it apart as a holy day.
Hebrews 4:9-11 NIV, Hebrews 3:12 NIV, Exodus 20:8-11 MSG

Friday

COVID Couldn't Stop All Saints

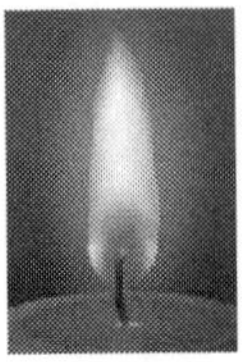

"The World Needs More Saints!"

So cries the humongous billboard in Albany, New York on behalf of a local recruitment campaign for Siena College whose mascot is a saint.

It happened to be up there on "All Saints Day."

Sometimes, we must be reminded as dramatically as that sign regarding our identity:

"To those sanctified in Christ Jesus, <u>called to be saints</u> together with all those who in every place call upon the name of our Lord Jesus Christ, both their Lord and ours..." (1 Corinthians 1:2)

If we stub our toe, burn the toast or make a very large and very bad investment, we call ourselves names.

But that is not who we are.

The word "saint" comes from the Greek word *hagios*, which means "consecrated to God, holy, sacred, pious."

COVID seemed to bring out The Saints like a football team being introduced to the stadium at the beginning of a game. The Body of Christ sprung into action during the pandemic because we identify with

Jesus.

Whenever you get into a fender bender or get a traffic ticket and need to give the officer your driver's license, just be sure to insert the word 'Hagios' before your first name. The policeman just may give you a pass…well, maybe.

PORTAL TO HEAVEN: Saints Alive. How we might interpret everything a little different if we were sure we were saints eternally.

But know that the Lord has set apart the godly man for Himself; The Lord hears when I call to Him...that is, the mystery which has been hidden from the past ages and generations, but has now been manifested to His saints...
Psalm 4:3 NASB, Colossians 1:26 NASB

Saturday

Was God Still King During COVID & The Election Cycle?

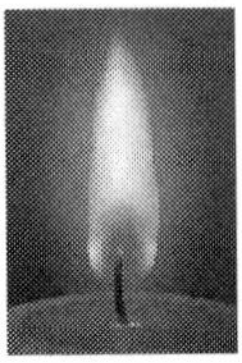

Was there a systematic and progressive jinx on the year 2020?

First, it's COVID. Then, economic fallout. Next, riots.

Finally, America needed help tying our political laces.

Some would call such an unfortunate series , "Unprecedented!"

But how would they know? Were these alive for Noah's flood or when Jerusalem or Rome were sacked or when Hitler was marching into France or ...

Evidently, others have experienced tragedy in the past and the pandemic is assuring children around the world that they will have stories for their grandchildren.

Like individuals who have gone through the hardest of times, America still stands after the election of 2020. At least, for now.

For those of us who sit in the recliner called "The U.S.A.," we may have finally been moved to the realization that a country cannot act as a substitute for God. No nation has ever escaped the collapse of its empire and America will eventually suffer the same fate if it has not already.

The year 2020 saw us elect thousands of leaders at every level. The real question is whether America will elect to be one nation...under God.

PORTAL TO HEAVEN: Crises reveal what's inside of us and portals open up when we determine to turn our hearts to God rather than to humans.

Godless nations rant and rave, kings and kingdoms threaten, but Earth

does anything he says...God is our refuge and strength, an ever-present help in trouble.Therefore we will not fear, though the earth give way and the mountains fall into the heart of the sea, though its waters roar and foam and the mountains quake with their surging. There is a river whose streams make glad the city of God, the holy place where the Most High dwells. God is within her, she will not fall; God will help her at break of day.Nations are in uproar, kingdoms fall; he lifts his voice, the earth melts.The Lord Almighty is with us; the God of Jacob is our fortress. Come and see what the Lord has done, the desolations he has brought on the earth. He makes wars cease to the ends of the earth. He breaks the bow and shatters the spear; he burns the shields with fire. He says, "Be still, and know that I am God; I will be exalted among the nations, I will be exalted in the earth."The Lord Almighty is with us; the God of Jacob is our fortress...And the Lord said to Samuel, "Obey the voice of the people in all that they say to you, for they have not rejected you, but they have rejected me from being king over them...Blessed is the nation whose God is the LORD, the people whom he has chosen as his heritage!

Psalm 46:6 MSG, Psalm 46 NIV, 1 Samuel 8:7, Psalm 33:12 ESV

4
Winter

The Candle & Season of Love

It Was a Cold, COVID Night...

We don't know exactly why God picked the timing for the first Christmas, but it's clear there seemed to be a long inter-testament period from The Old Testament's last prophet to the original prophet, Jesus Christ The Incarnate.

For many, the year 2020 will also be remembered for its slowness; that the messiah-like vaccine took forever to show up and free us from isolation and fear.

Two thousand years ago, God's chosen people felt distanced from their creator and were bound to the "lockdown" of Roman rule.

It is said that the pandemic of 2020 changed the world for good...or should we say, for bad...or should we say for good?

However one views COVID, the one thing that all will agree on was that there was a darkness that seemed to hover every culture and nation. But Christmas is all about light.

Christmas 2020 may well go as the most memorable one in our lifetime because COVID couldn't stop Christmas nor The Light of the World.

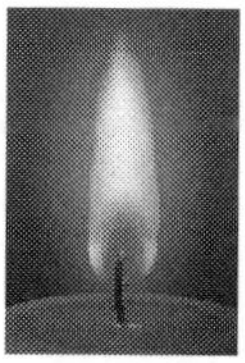

Putting The Unchangeables Into Your Own Words...

COVID Couldn't & The Covenant-Keeper

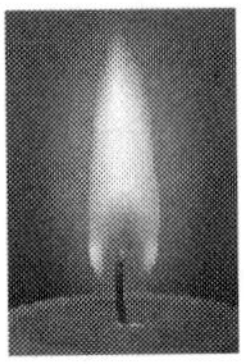

Part I
The First Coming

What could Christmas 2020 and Christmas 0000 have in common?

It's a riddle that would be easily answered by nine year olds in a Sunday school class.

"Jesus, Mary and Joseph!" they might answer.

In a word, "Family."

The first Christmas made it possible for anyone to become a member of God's family if they so chose. That offer still stands in 2020.

Whenever a country or culture goes through a dark period, it seems like an eternity before freedom is won. During the interim, however, important things become the focus.

The year 2020 will go down as being slow as a nine year old's wait on Christmas Eve.

For children who are brought up to know the real meaning of Christmas, their eyes are open to more than presents. Years after they have forgotten what they unwrapped, they will remember the greatest gift was the first family and the parents and siblings they were given. Sometimes, that takes an eternity to discover.

For those who embraced relationships during the lockdowns, it was like Yuletide every morning. By God's grace, it didn't take forever to awaken to that early and year-long Christmas present.

PORTAL TO HEAVEN: Families are representative of heaven where limitless relatives we call "saints" will forever enjoy each other's company without the coercion of something like COVID.

The people walking in darkness have seen a great light; on those living in the land of deep darkness a light has dawned...After this I looked, and there before me was a great multitude that no one could count, from every nation, tribe, people and language, standing before the throne and before the Lamb. They were wearing white robes and were holding palm branches in their hands. And they cried out in a loud voice: "Salvation belongs to our God, who sits on the throne, and to the Lamb."
Isaiah 9:2 NIV, Revelation 7:9,10 NIV

Monday

COVID Couldn't & The Covenant-Keeper

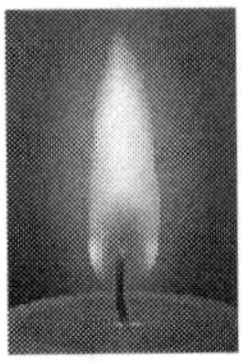

Part II

"Till death do us part..."

Wedding covenants were probably put in place because of passion...and problems.

Every marriage runs into walls — sometimes as rapidly as the honeymoon!

To scale such difficulties seems impossible for many and before long a lengthy document is detailing their divorce.

"Till death do us part" is one covenant in which Jesus has already done His part. The cross is the crowning example of a groom laying down His life all the way to the end. Will He not then keep His covenant to return?

Now, and through a couple of millennia, He has asked that His bride do to her part: to stay covenanted with Him until He returns.

The longings brought on by the pandemic's postponement of wedding vows is a magnificent metaphor for the Bride of Christ.

PORTAL TO HEAVEN: We are not alone in our yearning for Jesus' return. He is even more the eager.

Let us rejoice and be glad and give him glory! For the wedding of the Lamb has come, and his bride has made herself ready...He who did not spare his own Son, but gave him up for us all--how will he not also, along with him, graciously give us all things?... The Spirit and the bride say, "Come." And let the one who hears say, "Come."
Revelation 19:7 NIV, Romans 8:32 NIV, Revelation 22:17 NASB

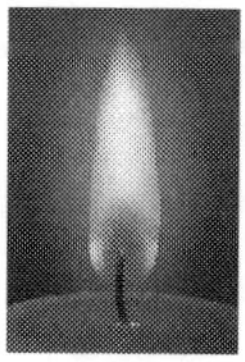

Putting The Unchangeables Into Your Own Words...

Tuesday

COVID Couldn't Stop Wise Men

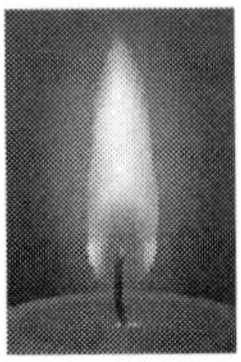

It seemed like the longest metaphorical walk for all contemporary wise men to get to Christmas, 2020.

Even the name, "Christmas 2020," may well become proverbial in its association with drawn-out journeys.

If people had to choose a few items to keep during COVID time, it would be anti-inflammatory medicines because that is one of the awful results of the coronavirus.

Another handy item might be gold in an era rife with uncertain economic times. After all, who hasn't seen a television commercial for gold during the pandemic?

It's interesting to note that the Wise Men came with frankincense and myrrh which are known for their anti-inflammatory properties and with gold and those gifts may have played a part in the safe passage of Joseph and Mary's journey to Egypt and back.

Whether unwitting or not, these travelers worshipped with practical presents as well as with their ageless and seemingly endless journey of adoration.

May that be said of the gifts we bring to The Baby well after the longest walk of COVID.

PORTAL TO HEAVEN: The pandemic "offerings" of God's people are portals to heaven for the unbeliever.

We want you to know about the grace that God has given the Macedonian churches. In the midst of a very severe trial, their overflowing joy and their extreme poverty welled up in rich generosity. For I testify that they gave as much as they were able, and even beyond their ability...How I praise the Lord that you are

concerned about me again. I know you have always beenconcerned for me, but you didn't have the chance to help me...they presented gifts to Him: gold, frankincense, and myrrh.
2 Corinthians 8:1-3 NIV, Philippians 4:10 NLT, Matthew 2:12 NKJV

Wednesday

COVID & Wise Men Who Still Seek Him

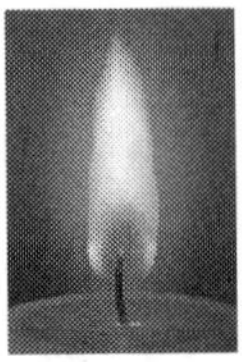

Luxury cars might make in hours or days the same arduous trip that took weeks for The Wise Men's camels.

To their credit, the trio stayed the course in an era of Roman occupation, Herodian corrupt rulership and unpredictable economic times.

The danger, travel and wit of the trio give us an indication of how devoted they were to God and His mysterious timeline.

The year 2020 may well go down in history as one of those pivotal years when people traveled through their anxieties, illnesses and harsh financial burdens in order to get to Jesus.

The test to see if these same weary contemporary sojourners truly met the Christmas Babe will be whether or not they, like the Wise Men, went home a different way than they came and whether their cars, luxury or otherwise, might affirm their gratitude by sporting a bumper sticker that says, "Wise men still seek Him."

PORTAL TO HEAVEN: It sometimes takes the blackest sky to highlight the brightest star.

Now after Jesus was born in Bethlehem of Judea in the days of Herod the king, behold, wise men from the East came to Jerusalem..."we have seen His star in the East and have come to worship Him."...Then, being divinely warned in a dream that they should not return to Herod, they departed for their own country another way.

Matthew 2:1,2,12 NKJV

Christmas Eve

The Longest Night

The longest night for a child is Christmas Eve.

The longest 'night' for adults has been the lockdown of 2020.

It has been painful to watch seniors respond to COVID. Many have lived through World War II, 911 and personal tragedies. They are worn out and anxious to get on with life. They fear the world will never be the same.

But even those who have not witnessed the great wars are anxiety-ridden with the thought that life will never be the same.

So, they wait. They listen to media reports. They wait for vaccines.

Who is putting us through this? Is it God?

Wait a minute! Have we not put The Holy Trinity through the very longest 'night?' Millenia of sin, selfishness and stubbornness led to The Son expiring as He envisioned the "joy set before Him." (Hebrews 12:2 NIV)

His patience is without precedence.

May every waking adult be childlike as we wait not just for a temporal vaccine, but for the culmination of Christmas.

PORTAL TO HEAVEN: Patience that is passed down can transition into a peaceful expectancy.

Let us fix our eyes on Jesus, the author and perfecter of our faith, who for the joy set before Him endured the cross, scorning its shame, and sat down at the right hand of the throne of God...My Father's house has many rooms; if that were not so, would I have told you that I am going there to prepare a place for you?
Hebrews 12:2 BSB, Matthew 14:12 NIV

Stable Stability

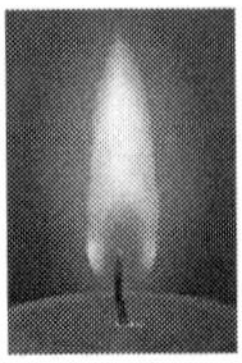

Everyone loves stability. The year 2020 offered none.

If the pandemic were to close all of the malls, would Christmas be Christmas? If the family and friends we so dearly missed during 2020 were still unreachable during the holidays, would Christmas be Christmas? If countries were turned upside down by unrest and political upheaval, would Christmas be Christmas?

The theology of temporal stability is not one that the Baby Jesus experienced.

His ever-changing world began shortly after Christmas when he was shuttled to Egypt in the middle of the night. He probably wailed. After that, he was brought back to Israel only to be redirected to Nazareth. As an adult, he shuffled from one town to another, was run out of others and didn't seem to stay at any high-end hotels or pricey bed-and-breakfast stops.

On his last day, he shifted constantly on the instability of a few nails.

The first Christmas had some sort of stable and that was stable enough for God.

PORTAL TO HEAVEN: The most stable place in the world is still the breast of Jesus Christ.

And she brought forth her firstborn Son, and wrapped Him in swaddling cloths, and laid Him in a manger, because there was no room for them in the inn...Seeing was believing. [The shepherds] told everyone they met what the angels had said about this child... With my own eyes I've seen your salvation; it's now out in the open for everyone to see:...There was reclining on Jesus' bosom one of His disciples, whom Jesus loved.
Luke 2:7 NKJV, Luke 2:17,18,31 MSG, John 13:23 NASB. Editor's brackets.

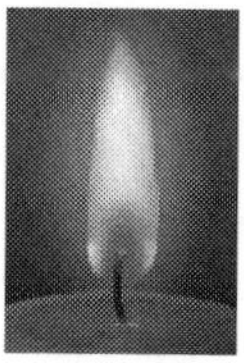

Putting The Unchangeables Into Your Own Words...

About the Author

Robert J. LaCosta, the songwriter of LOVE GOES VIRAL, is a prolific writer who has penned books, screenplays, thousands of songs, children's stories, newspaper and magazine columns on "Retiring Retirement." He continues a daily online devotional called "Portals to Heaven."

His career in the field of hearing aids inspired him to help people hear in the spiritual realm and use their natural senses to discover the supernatural "hints" that God throws our way in-the-moment to reassure us of His great and personal love.

Learning to use what he has coined the "metaphor-du-jour" is a key in discovering daily portals that cement the idea that the Holy Spirit is ever-present and the fulfillment of the closeness of Jesus Christ, Emmanuel, which means "God with us."

His teachings and live and recorded music have blessed thousands.

LaCosta and his wife Vini have a combined four children and three grandchildren and live in Upstate New York alongside the historic and scenic Hudson River.

More Works By The Author

robertlacosta.com

All of these impacting creative works make meaningful presents and help support worthy organizations.

Books

Like Father, Like Son

The King's Favorite Book • A StoryJournal™

Gamaliel's Advice

Portals to Heaven • Learning the 'Metaphor-du-Jour'

Dodging Death For a Living

Screenplays*:

Gamaliel's Advice - Taking Down God
(based on the Mt. Soledad Cross)

Kidnapping Chris

Albums & EP's:

Love Goes Viral

I Want To Be Part of a Miracle

My Day Will Be My Act of Worship

I Want To Hear

He Stood For Me

365 - Does That Make Today Christmas Day?

Magazine Contributor:
Family Now: 'Retiring Retirement'

**We are actively looking for those who want to impact the world by financially helping get these works to screen.*

Printed in Great Britain
by Amazon

50439156R00038